For Malala...

A Wreath of Sonnets

Poems by Patricia Maynard

Cover Art by Jordan Avery

About this art form:

A sonnet is a fourteen line rhymed poem written in iambic pentameter.

A crown of sonnets is a group of fourteen sonnets, written on different themes of a common subject, with the last line of the first becoming the first line of the second, and so on.

A heroic crown of sonnets has a fifteenth sonnet made up on the first lines of the first fourteen.

A wreath of sonnets is a heroic crown, with the last poem containing an acrostic in which the first letters of each line create a phrase.

This wreath of sonnets was inspired by the efforts of Malala Yousafzai, a young Pakistani woman who has been a voice, despite great obstacles, for the education of all. Her message has continued to echo across the world.

Sonnet # 1

Can one whose life began so far away

Influence a culture from a different sphere,

Where freedom is accepted, a cliché,

The background for decisions without fear.

They take for granted opportunities

To learn, to work, to play without restraint.

No chance authoritarian decrees

Will squelch their lives and stifle all complaint.

So unaware that others are denied

The chance of books and pens for everyone,

They can't imagine prayers that have been cried,

Or bullets taken on a bus toward home.

These lines are here that we (on her behalf)

Remember now the struggles on the path.

Sonnet # 2

Remember now the struggles on the path

As edicts flew and rights were tossed aside.

The guns, the threats, the nightmares of blood baths,

The sacrifices made by those who died.

No females on the streets may show your face--

No colors in your dresses except black—

No school for girls—you will stay in your place--

Go home, stay put, and don't you dare look back!

But bullets cannot stop the single voice

Who dares to whisper no while others shout,

Who knows the value of maintaining choice,

Who keeps believing while the others doubt.

There's one determined she will find a way

Out of the scattered remnants of a day.

Sonnet # 3

Out of the scattered remnants of a day,

She finds the pieces of a broken dream,

And fits them back together in a way

The picture in the puzzle can be seen.

Some do endure an interrupted life,

Emerging with a strength that's been renewed.

Awareness can be crystallized by strife,

And colors be reborn with vivid hues.

Where one might sink, another rises strong,

Rejects restrictions meant to hold her down,

Commits herself to singing her true song—

This tree won't quietly fall without a sound.

She transcends what would stop her in her path.

When fates were thrust into the arms of wrath.

Sonnet # 4

When fates were thrust into the arms of wrath
There was no place to duck, nowhere to hide,
No one to take the pain on her behalf,
Yet this young life would not be here denied.
Descending where she'd hidden from the pain,
She hoped for miracles to then emerge
To counteract a force that seemed profane
And send the healing muses to converge.
The surgeons' skill, the medicines, the sleep,
Her body stitched together like a doll,
She found her spirit touchstone in the deep
Refusing every chance to take the fall.
She longed to see in dreams of reverence
New faces that were full of innocence.

Sonnet # 5

New faces that were full of innocence

Look on in stunned and desperate disbelief.

Restrictions are imposed that make no sense

To steal away their choices like a thief.

Societies all discriminate by race,

By gender, money, lover, how to pray.

The hope is that ideals that some embrace

Inspire equality for every way.

Denied free will means they're denied their dreams,

No means of taking back what they have lost,

No shields against the angry vivid streams

Toward those who randomly must pay the cost.

They fear they'll live forever in a cage,

Forever wear the scars of focused rage.

Sonnet # 6

Forever wear the scars of focused rage?

A martyr is not what she has in mind.

She tries to watch, to understand, to gauge

The fears that seem to motivate mankind.

For surely such controlling needs have roots

In paranoid projections planted deep,

That any deviation at the foot

Will bring down all creation in a heap.

They keep the spirit trimmed, cut back, and pruned,

As if a child or woman could be tamed

Into a creature who's been finely tuned

To live in shadows, choices always framed.

She wonders at the seeds and sustenance

Of fear that spawned a desperate violence.

Sonnet # 7

Of fear that spawned a desperate violence
Are roots embedded deep in rigid thought.
All motivations spiral from a sense
Of danger that their way of life is caught
In threats that would destroy their core beliefs,
That there is only one way to live right,
And rules are made to offer them relief
From possibilities not in their sight.
Extremists from all corners seem to think
That limits, judgments, laws are put in place
To keep them from temptations at the brink
Of evil with the power to erase
Their world's ideals, a war they fight on stage,
Refusing even now to turn the page.

Sonnet # 8

Refusing even now to turn the page,

He clings to old traditions stubbornly,

Denies ideas of progress, cannot gauge

The obsolescence others freely see.

The hammer seems to be his only tool

To strike whatever challenges his way.

He's not afraid to leave a bloody pool,

A wake behind his ignorance this day.

He fires his bullets in a school girls' bus,

Deluded that his act protects belief.

But all who seek what's true, who seek what's just

Will know him as they say their prayers of grief.

May be imprisoned minds can be set free;

May be the one who should be blind can see.

Sonnet # 9

May be the one who should be blind can see,

Appreciating views that others miss.

A brush with loss enhances sensory

Perceptions and intensity persists.

Awareness is more keen, an altered state

We wish we could maintain on quiet days.

But time has veiled our consciousness of late

Unless we still our minds to clear the haze.

Some call it meditation, and some, prayer,

Some seek within, some seek a higher being.

And all who wish to tend this world with care

Will be rewarded with a deeper seeing.

The one who pays attention is aware

And one who should be deaf can hear the prayer.

Sonnet #10

The one who should be deaf can hear the prayer
Because she knows to listen from the heart,
A gift that sounds so easy, but is rare
Since people's thoughts sometimes set them apart.
Somehow she knows that separateness is false,
Illusions that we're different interfere
And knowledge of atonement is not sought
When human ties that bind us disappear.
Her losses mount—her school, her home, her place—
She still resists the bitterness of hate.
Her scars will heal, she'll choose to show her face
And look not up, not down, but open, straight.
She senses shackles that she cannot see
Loss can eventually give way to free.

Sonnet # 11

Loss can eventually give way to free

A spirit from possessions and from fear,

But all beings do need opportunities

To strengthen, stretch, go limitless from here.

To be denied the basic right to learn

Reduces life's experiences to bones,

Such lost abilities then to discern—

Fulfillment from existence stays unknown.

She feels she needs some say-so in her fate

(Although control's illusion after all).

It's not enough to watch, obey, and wait—

She must respond in answer to the call.

Her new perspective prompts her to declare

A will to serve, a salient voice to share.

Sonnet # 12

A will to serve, a salient voice to share—
That drop of water wears away the stone.
When love and truth and constancy are there
Our destiny looms spheres beyond this one.
In theory, butterflies can spread their wings
And alter weather patterns miles away.
When unrestricted voices join to sing,
Resulting harmonies are born to stay.
The individual force can guide the herd.
Some call her agent, rallying for change,
Some call her traitor, and her ways absurd,
Reacting as if she's the one deranged.
And still she gives a strong idea rebirth:
Less fear, less anger fuel the deeds of worth.

Sonnet #13

Less fear, less anger fuel the deeds of worth.

Connections spring from empathy and trust.

The holy motivator is toward growth,

For otherwise, we run the risk of rust.

Religions can't excuse a vicious bent.

(And surely we've evolved since old crusades?)

It's faith that will provide encouragement

To seek the light and love that cannot fade.

Although they risk exposure to the rod,

They are not scared to seek the source of truth.

There is no holy war: God is not God

Who directs murder, targeting our youth.

Enlightened hearts will seek this truth from birth,

That love's the force of reckoning on earth.

Sonnet #14

That love's the force of reckoning on earth
Is proven when forgiveness inspires peace,
When those who suffer shift into rebirth,
When hungers for revenge and payback cease.
The prophets, mystics, poets all agree
That darkness fueled by ignorance and fear
Is lit by knowledge, service, charity—
The learner's ready; teachers will appear.
The bombs and bullets will not kill the word,
Nor desperate acts of violence still the voice.
Her courage, grace, and vision now will stir
A world to act in ways that honor choice.
Can each of us join in this choir today?
Can one whose life began so far away?

Sonnet # 15

Can one whose life began so far away

Remember now the struggles on the path,

Out of the scattered remnants of a day

When fates were thrust into the arms of wrath?

New faces that were full of innocence

Forever wear the scars of focused rage,

Of fear that spawned a desperate violence,

Refusing even now to turn the page.

May be the one who should be blind can see

And one who should be deaf can hear the prayer.

Loss can eventually give way to free

A will to serve, a salient voice to share.

Less fear, less anger fuel the deeds of worth

And love's the force of reckoning on earth.

www.ingramcontent.com/pod-product-compliance
Lightning Source LLC
Chambersburg PA
CBHW070829100426
42813CB00003B/550